P9-CDI-994

High? Low? Where Did It Go?

I'm the Cat in the Hat.
Come and travel with me
to find animals that
are not easy to see.

The Cat in the Hat's Learning Library®
introduces beginning readers to basic non-fiction. If your child can read these lines, then he or she can begin to understand the fascinating world in which we live.

Learn to read. Read to learn.

This book comes from the home of

THE CAT IN THE HAT

RANDOM HOUSE

For a list of books in **The Cat in the Hat's Learning Library**, *see the back endpaper.*

To all my friends at
Reach Out and Read, with love
—T.R.

The editors would like to thank
BARBARA KIEFER, Ph.D.,
Charlotte S. Huck Professor of Children's Literature,
The Ohio State University, and
JIM BREHENY,
Director, Bronx Zoo,
for their assistance in the preparation of this book.

Visit us on the Web!
Seussville.com
randomhousekids.com

Educators and librarians, for a variety of teaching tools, visit us at RHTeachersLibrarians.com

Library of Congress Cataloging-in-Publication Data
Rabe, Tish, author.
High? low? where did it go? : all about animal camouflage / by Tish Rabe ; illustrated by
Aristides Ruiz and Joe Mathieu.
  pages cm. — (The Cat in the Hat's learning library)
Summary: "The Cat in the Hat introduces young readers to the concept of camouflage—a type of
adaptation that helps animals survive." —Provided by publisher.
Audience: Ages 5–8.
ISBN 978-0-449-81496-3 (trade) — ISBN 978-0-375-97169-3 (lib. bdg.)
1. Camouflage (Biology)—Juvenile literature. 2. Protective coloration (Biology)—Juvenile
literature. 3. Animals—Color—Juvenile literature. 4. Animal behavior—Juvenile literature.
I. Ruiz, Aristides, ill. II. Mathieu, Joe, ill. III. Title. IV. Series: Cat in the Hat's learning library.
QL767.R33 2016 591.47'2—dc23 2015018390

Printed in the United States of America   10 9 8 7 6 5 4 3 2 1

High? Low? Where Did It Go?

by Tish Rabe

illustrated by Aristides Ruiz and Joe Mathieu

The Cat in the Hat's Learning Library®

Random House 🏠 New York

I'm the Cat in the Hat.
Come and travel with me
to find animals that
are not easy to see.

Camouflage helps them hide.
It's the way they're concealed,
but these hidden animals
will soon be revealed!

All over the world,
animals must adapt
to the conditions
of their habitat.

Adaptations are traits
that help animals survive—
different looks or behaviors
that keep them alive.

An example is camouflage,
which helps to protect them.
If they cannot be seen,
others may not detect them.

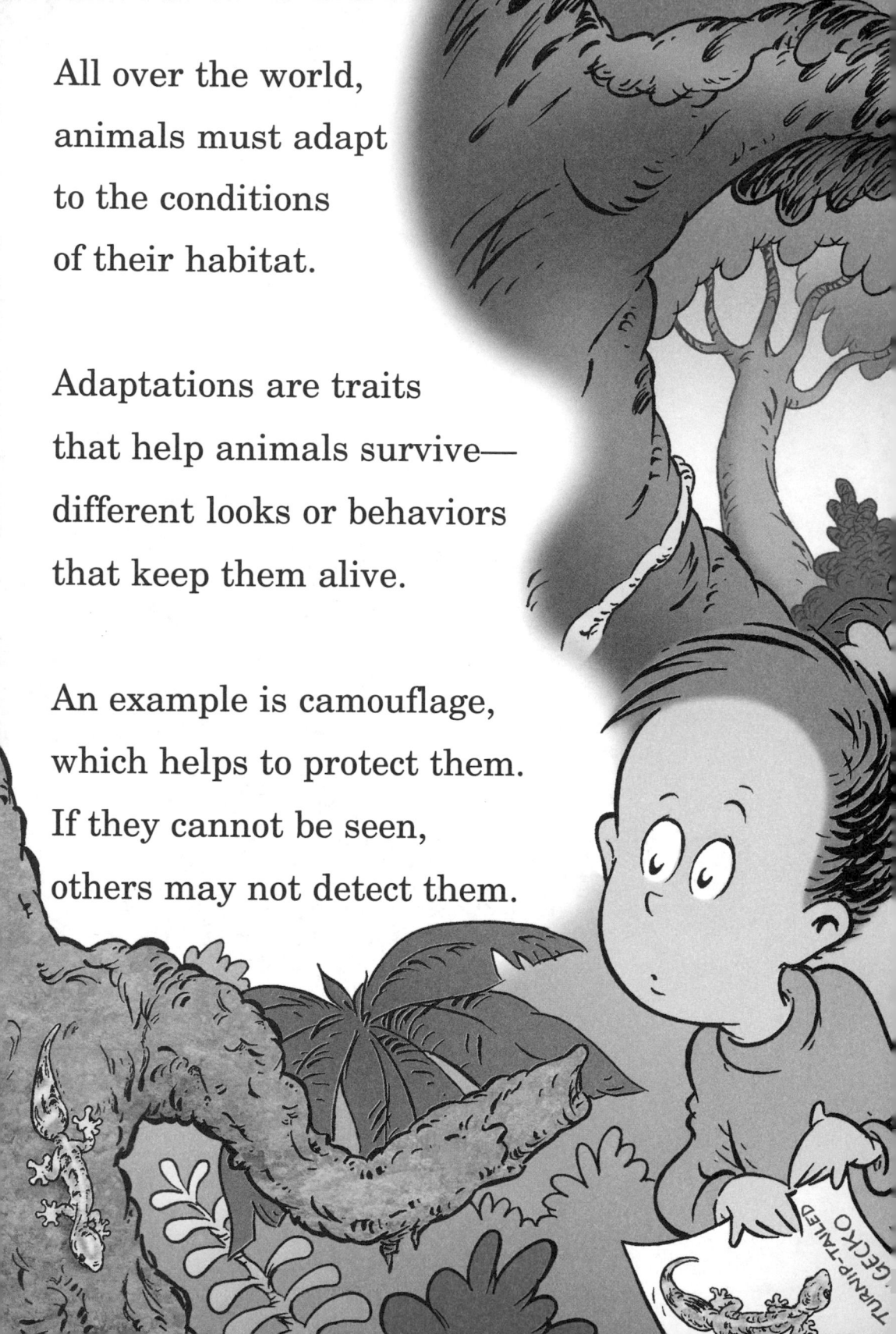

There are different kinds of camouflage adaptation. This first one is called **concealing coloration.**

Some animals change color to match their background. It helps them blend in so they may not be found.

Concealing coloration is a type of camouflage.

During the winter, this little stoat blends in with the snow with its fluffy white coat.

In the spring, it will grow a new coat that is brown so it can blend in with colors on the ground.

This sloth barely moves.
When he does, he's so slow
that on his shaggy fur
some plants start to grow!

These plants are called algae.
They turn his fur green.
He blends in with the leaves
and can hardly be seen!

Some animals change color
when danger is near.
Predators may not
even know they are here.

These are flashlight fish.
Watch as they swim by.
They have glowing bacteria
under each eye.

These bacteria let out
a bright greenish glow,
which lights up dark water
wherever they go.

But when they're in danger,
small folds in their skin
cover the glow
so the fish can blend in.

Some animals hide
right in front of our eyes.
They are hard to see
'cause they wear a **disguise**!

To keep hidden, some look
just like things they are not.
It's the reason why
they're not easy to spot.

This leafy sea dragon
floats in the ocean.
It looks like seaweed
as it moves in slow motion.

LEAFY SEA DRAGON

DISGUISE IS A TYPE OF CAMOUFLAGE.

t's hard to believe when
ou're watching it swish
hat it isn't seaweed—
t's really a fish!

This violet snail
can hide easily.
It makes bubbles and looks
just like foam on the sea.

This flounder looks just like
the rocky seabed.
We see only its eyes
on the side of its head.

cuba dive in the ocean,
nd you may get a shock!
he poisonous stonefish
oks just like a rock!

The insect on this tree
has a life-saving trick.
Instead of an insect,
it looks like a stick!

WALKING
STICK

20

Sticks do not run, so
when threatened, it will
stop where it is
and then stay very still.

Some animals need
to sneak up on their prey.
(If they're seen by prey,
the prey may get away!)

Alligators look like logs.
They sit and they wait.
Prey don't know they're in danger
until it's too late!

An eyelash viper
and this fruit look alike.
The snake hides in the fruit
till it's ready to strike!

EYELASH
VIPER

This next kind of camouflage adaptation Thing One says is called **disruptive coloration**.

Some animals have markings like stripes, patches, and dots. Some have a few markings, but others have lots.

DISRUPTIVE COLORATION IS A TYPE OF CAMOUFLAGE.

Markings help hide their shape.
Is this tiger big or small?
Its stripes hide it so we
can't see its shape at all.

This little fawn has
white dots on her fur.
In a field of white flowers,
it's hard to see her.

While mother finds food,
she leaves her fawn behind.
The fawn's markings protect her.
She's not easy to find.

A bittern's feathers are striped
and that's what it needs,
to keep undercover and
hide in the reeds.

When wind hits the reeds,
the bird sways side to side.
Its stripes look like the reeds,
and that helps it to hide.

BITTERN

Zebras travel in herds.
Their stripes blend in, like these—
the patterns help zebras
confuse enemies.

This baby zebra
stays close to her mother.
Their stripes blend so it's hard
to tell one from the other.

A lion moves in
but can't tell them apart.
Where does mother end?
Where does baby start?

To stay safe, some animals
use this survival trick—
they **mimic** other animals
that make predators sick.

A bird gets sick if it eats
a monarch butterfly,
so it won't try to catch one.
It lets monarchs fly by.

MONARCH

VICEROY

Viceroys look like monarchs, which make birds sick, and so birds don't catch viceroys either. They just let them go.

MIMICRY IS A TYPE OF CAMOUFLAGE.

MIMICRY IS A KIND OF CAMOUFLAGE.

Countershading makes some animals "disappear," helping them to survive— like this penguin right here.

Penguins have dark backs, but their bellies are light. When they swim, this shading helps them stay out of sight.

If a leopard seal looks DOWN when the penguin starts to swim, his dark back blends in so the seal can't see him.

COUNTERSHADING IS A TYPE OF CAMOUFLAGE.

And if a killer whale looks UP,
the penguin fades out of sight.
He blends in with the sky
because his belly is white.

Some animals hide in things that surround them. They "dress up" in what they can find all around them.

To stay hidden, an Australian tailor ant weaves a nest for itself out of still-growing leaves.

The leaves keep on growing
in front of and behind it,
which may make it hard for
a predator to find it.

This crab covers itself
in seaweed decoration
that falls off when it moves
to another location.

When it gets to a new place,
what this crab must do
is cover up with more seaweed
to stay hidden from view.

DECORATOR CRAB

Camouflaged animals play
hide-and-seek day and night.
To survive and find food,
they must stay out of sight.

They spend their whole lives
trying to disappear.
Can you find ten of them?
They are hiding right here!

Answer on
page 45

GLOSSARY

Adaptation: A change of form or behavior to survive in different surroundings.

Algae: Tiny plant without roots, stems, or leaves.

Camouflage: The hiding of things so they cannot be seen or recognized easily.

Conceal: To hide or cover from sight.

Countershading: A form of camouflage in which some parts of an animal's body are dark and some are light.

Disguise: To change appearance in order to hide.

Disruptive: Causing separation or division into different parts.

Habitat: The place where a person or thing is usually found.

Mimic: To copy or be like something else.

Predator: An animal that lives by capturing and eating other animals.

Prey: An animal that is hunted by other animals for food.

Reveal: To uncover or allow to be seen.

Scuba: Equipment worn by divers for breathing underwater.

Trait: A distinct or different feature or quality.

FOR FURTHER READING

101 Hidden Animals by Melvin and Gilda Berger (Scholastic). Fun facts and photos of amazing camouflaged animals. For grades two and up.

How to Hide an Octopus and Other Sea Creatures by Ruth Heller (Grosset & Dunlap, *Reading Railroad Books*). Realistic illustrations and simple, rhyming text introduce young readers to camouflaged sea creatures. Other books in the series include *How to Hide a Butterfly and Other Insects* and *How to Hide a Crocodile and Other Reptiles*. For preschool and up.

What Color Is Camouflage? by Carolyn Otto, illustrated by Megan Lloyd (HarperTrophy, *Let's-Read-and-Find-Out Science*®, Stage 2). A simple introduction to how and why different animals use camouflage. For kindergarten and up.

Where in the Wild? Camouflaged Creatures Concealed . . . and Revealed by David M. Schwartz and Yael Schy, with photographs by Dwight Kuhn (Tricycle Press). This unique book, an NSTA-CBC Outstanding Science Trade Book for Children, combines artful photographs of camouflaged animals with poems that give clues to their identities. For preschool and up.

INDEX

Camouflaged animals play
hide-and-seek day and night.
To survive and find food,
they must stay out of sight.

They spend their whole lives
trying to disappear.
Can you find ten of them?
They are hiding right here!

The Cat in the Hat's Learning Library®

Can You See a Chimpanzee?

Clam-I-Am!

Fine Feathered Friends

A Great Day for Pup

Hark! A Shark!

High? Low? Where Did It Go?

Hurray for Today!

I Can Name 50 Trees Today!

Ice Is Nice!

If I Ran the Dog Show

If I Ran the Horse Show

If I Ran the Rain Forest

Inside Your Outside!

Is a Camel a Mammal?

Miles and Miles of Reptiles

My, Oh My—a Butterfly!

Oh Say Can You Say DI-NO-SAUR?

Oh Say Can You Say What's the Weather Today?

Oh Say Can You Seed?

Oh, the Pets You Can Get!

Oh, the Things They Invented!

Oh, the Things You Can Do That Are Good for You!

On Beyond Bugs!

Once upon a Mastodon

One Cent, Two Cents, Old Cent, New Cent

Out of Sight Till Tonight!

Safari, So Good!

There's a Map on My Lap!

There's No Place Like Space!

A Whale of a Tale!

What Cat Is That?

Why Oh Why Are Deserts Dry?

Wish for a Fish

Would You Rather Be a Pollywog?

Coming in 2016:

One Vote, Two Votes, I Vote, You Vote